Our World of Information

Sort It Out

Choosing Information

Claire Throp

Heinemann Library,
Chicago, IL

www.heinemannraintree.com
Visit our website to find out more information about Heinemann-Raintree books.

To order:

 Phone 888-454-2279
Visit www.heinemannraintree.com to browse our catalog and order online.

Edited by Rebecca Rissman and Catherine Veitch
Designed by Richard Parker
Original illustrations © Capstone Global Library
Illustrated by Darren Lingard
Picture research by Ruth Blair
Production by Duncan Gilbert
Originated by Heinemann Library
Printed in China by South China Printing Company Ltd.

14 13 12 11 10
10 9 8 7 6 5 4 3 2 1

Library of Congress Cataloging-in-Publication Data
Throp, Claire.
  Sort it out : choosing information / Claire Throp.
    p. cm. -- (Our world of information)
  Includes bibliographical references and index.
  ISBN 978-1-4329-3372-2 -- ISBN 978-1-4329-3378-4 (pbk.)
1. Information resources--Juvenile literature. 2. Information resources--Evaluation--Juvenile literature. I. Title.
  ZA3070.T485 2009
  020--dc22
                              2009004406

Acknowledgments

We would like to thank the following for permission to reproduce photographs: Alamy pp. **11** (© PhotoAlto), **18** (© Design Pics Inc.), **19** (© Pablo Paul), **22** (© Blend Images), **29** (© Jupiterimages/Goodshoot); © Capstone Publishers pp. **7, 13, 17, 23 & 28** (Karon Dubke); Corbis pp. **5** (Sean Justice), **8** (Image 100), **14** (Catherine Karnow), **27**; Getty Images pp. **6** (Blend Images), **21** (Sean Gallup); Photoshot pp. **9, 25** (Blend Images); Shutterstock p. **12** (© Underworld).

Cover photograph of a girl in a library with a laptop computer and book reproduced with permission of Punchstock (Brand X Pictures).

Every effort has been made to contact copyright holders of any material reproduced in this book. Any omissions will be rectified in subsequent printings if notice is given to the publisher.

All the Internet addresses (URLs) given in this book were valid at the time of going to press. However, due to the dynamic nature of the Internet, some addresses may have changed, or sites may have changed or ceased to exist since publication. While the author and publisher regret any inconvenience this may cause readers, no responsibility for any such changes can be accepted by either the author or the publisher.

Contents

Information All Around Us 4
How Do I Choose? 6
Understand the Assignment. 8
Which Information Can We Trust? . . 10
Books 12
Other Sources 14
Websites. 16
Understanding Information 18
Too Much Information! 20
A Range of Information 22
Keep a Record 24
What Comes Next?. 26
Activities. 28
Glossary. 30
Find Out More 31
Index 32

Any words appearing in the text in bold, **like this**, are explained in the glossary.

Information All Around Us

You are surrounded by information.
Information is what people know about things.
Information can be signs, pictures, or words
that tell you how to do things or where to go.

 Information can be found in books
and newspapers, on the Internet,
and by asking questions.

In your everyday life you often need to choose information from different **sources**. This book will help you to find out which information you need, whatever you are doing.

 Always be prepared to ask for help.

How Do I Choose?

The best way to choose which **source** of information to use depends on what you want the information for. For example, you might want to find out when a major-league baseball team is playing. Doing a search on the Internet should help you find the answer.

 You could also do a search using a cell phone.

If you have a new pet, you probably want to find out how to take care of it. You will have to figure out which sources provide the information you need. In this case, the Internet, books, and a vet will be good sources of information.

 A library is a good place to look for information.

Understand the Assignment

If you are choosing information for a school **project**, then the first thing to do is to make sure you understand the assignment. Then make a list of what you already know about the topic. What do you need to find out?

 If you are not sure exactly which **sources** are the best to use, ask your teacher or librarian to help you.

An **encyclopedia** can be a good place to start. If you need more precise information, you can look in other **reference books**. If you are not sure what you are looking for, go back to your topic. Make a list of possible **keywords** for an Internet search.

A print or **online** encyclopedia will give you general background information and an overview of the topic.

Which Information Can We Trust?

You can trust some **sources** more than others. This is because **facts** can get confused with **opinions**. Facts are what people know for sure about a topic. Facts are the same in different sources. Opinions are the feelings of one person or one group of people about a topic. Opinions cannot be proven.

 This boy has an opinion about carrots.

It is always good to read information for yourself, so that you know you can trust it.

You should also be careful about trusting information that people tell you. Someone may tell you about something they have heard or read, but you cannot always be sure that what they have told you is correct. People can twist the facts to match their opinions, or they may not understand your question.

Books

When did we land on the moon?

A _____
_____
_____
_____
_____
_____
_____
_____

 Is this book up-to-date?

Books are one of the most reliable **sources** of information. This is because they are usually carefully checked before they are **published**. **Experts** read the information inside books to make sure it is correct.

You should always check that books you use as sources are up-to-date. To find out if a book is up-to-date, look at when the book was published on the **imprint page**.

 The date a book was published is normally found on the imprint page of a book.

Other Sources

Printed **sources** of information include books, flyers, magazines, and newspapers. You can trust some newspapers or magazines more than others. National newspapers may have more **experts** checking the **facts** than a small local paper or school magazine.

Information in newspapers is usually up-to-date.

Opinion can sometimes get confused with fact on television and in radio programs. You should also be careful about information in **commercials**. Commercials are made by companies to encourage people to buy things. Their information may be one-sided, so you cannot completely trust it.

Websites

When you look for information on the Internet, you must be very careful. You cannot trust all the information you find. Some Websites are set up by people who are not **experts**. These Websites may include **opinions** rather than just **facts**.

Space website

Hi!
I am Mike. This is my very own web site. Iv'e learned all about the planets and that, and wont to share it with you all.

This is the moon. They sed it was made of cheeese cos its got lots of hole in it. The earth goes round and round it, and we only see it at night when its dark.

It is the nearest planet to the earth, and in the 1960s a guy called Buzz aldrin went there in a rockit with some other guys to see what was there, but they did not find nothing.

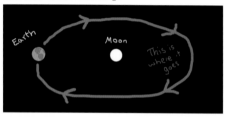

Here are two Websites about space. Which one would you trust?

It is best to use Websites that have been created by a well-known organization or the government. If you are not sure whether a Website is useful, you can check with a teacher or librarian.

 A lot of information can be found on the Internet, but not all of it can be trusted.

Understanding Information

During your search, you may come across information that is difficult to understand. This could be because it was written for older children or adults. Sometimes you can ask an adult to help you understand, but it is better to try to find **sources** aimed at your own age group.

Ask for help if you do not understand something.

If you are not sure the information you found is useful, try a simple test. Can you explain the information using your own words to a friend or someone in your class? If it seems too difficult then try another source.

Try to use sources of information that are the right level for your age group.

Too Much Information!

Some Websites are made especially for children. Others may have a special section for children.

Sometimes it is difficult to organize the information you have found because there is so much of it. You must take only what you need from the **sources** of information you have found.

Look back at your **project** or your topic. Sort out the information that helps you complete your assignment. Get rid of the information that does not help.

 Talk to friends about the information they have found.

A Range of Information

When you use a range of **sources**, you can **cross-check** your **facts**. This means that if you find a fact in one source and then find the same information in a different source, the fact is more likely to be correct.

 Some people believe that you should find the same information in three sources before you can be sure that it is correct.

When you look at a number of different sources, you need to be careful not to copy other people's work. Copying is stealing the work of another person. You should always put the information you find into your own words.

 Find information from different sources and then put it into your own words.

Keep a Record

You should always keep a record of the different **sources** you use when you search for information. Your record of sources will show your teacher where you have found your facts. A record can also tell others where to look to learn more about your topic.

 A librarian can help you find a source. He or she can also help you document your source.

Keep a list of useful information sources in case you want to use them again.

Your teacher may ask you to list the sources you have used at the end of a piece of schoolwork. That way your teacher can see what research you have done. Listing sources is also a way of thanking the person or group who provided the information.

What Comes Next?

Some information is good to share out loud.

The best **sources** of information will depend on the type of information you want to find. It will also depend on how you plan to use the information. Be aware of how you can trust some sources more than others.

Sorting out the information you have found can be hard work. However, once you have chosen the information you want to keep, the next step is to figure out how to use it.

 Information can be found in so many places that it can be confusing.

Activities

Making a Tourist Leaflet

Imagine a tourist is coming to visit your area. Design an information leaflet about where you live. Try finding three or four different **sources** of information. Choose the most useful information from each of the sources. Put the **facts** together into a leaflet, and do not forget to include pictures.

You could take photographs of a member of your family, a pet, or favorite toy.

Taking Photographs For a Poster

Use a digital camera to take some photographs. Then use a computer to look at the pictures and choose the best two or three to use. Make a poster of your pictures. Write two sentences about each photograph you have chosen.

Glossary

commercial made by companies to get people to buy the DVDs, toys, or other things they make. Information in commercials is usually one-sided.

cross-check checking a particular piece of information in a number of different sources

encyclopedia book with information about many subjects, or with a lot of information about a particular subject

expert person who has a lot of knowledge about a particular topic

fact something that is known for certain about a topic

imprint page page in a book that gives information about who helped to create the book and when it was written. An imprint page usually appears near the beginning of a book.

keyword word that describes the particular subject you want to find information about

online connected to the Internet

opinion thoughts and feelings about a topic that one person or group of people may have

project task set by a teacher that can be done on your own or with other people

published printed materials, such as books and magazines, produced for sale

reference book a book, such as a dictionary or encyclopedia, that you can use to find reliable information

source place in which we can find information. Books, television, and the Internet are sources of information.

Find Out More

Books

Doudna, Kelly. *I'll Use Information for My Explanation!* Edina, Minn.: ABDO Publishing, 2007.

Oxlade, Chris. *My First Internet Guide*. Chicago, Ill.: Heinemann Library, 2007.

Websites

Homework Help – Yahoo! Kids
http://kids.yahoo.com/learn
This web page includes links to an encyclopedia, dictionary, maps, and a lot of other useful Websites.

CBBC – Stay Safe
www.bbc.co.uk/cbbc/help/safesurfing
This Website gives you advice on staying safe while you are on the Internet.

Index

books 4, 7, 9, 12–13, 14

cell phones 6
commercials 15
copying 23
cross-checking 22

encyclopedias 9
experts 12, 14, 16

facts 10, 11, 14, 15, 16, 22

imprint page 13
Internet 4, 6, 7, 9, 16–17, 20

keywords 9

libraries 7, 24

newspapers and
    magazines 4, 14

online information 9,
    16–17, 20
opinions 10, 11, 15, 16
organizing information
    20–21, 27

projects 8, 21

questions 8, 9, 11

record of sources 24, 25
reference books 9

sources of information 5, 6,
    7, 10, 12, 14, 15, 18, 19,
    20, 22, 23, 24, 25, 26, 28

television and radio 15
trusting information 10–11,
    15, 17, 26

understanding information
    18–19

Websites 16–17, 20